Self Publish on

CreateSpace at

Zero Cost

Part of the Zero Cost Self Publishing Series.
Publish and distribute to the world at zero cost.

3rd Edition

by

Stephen C Norton

A Northwind Ink Publication

as always

For Gail

Books by the Author

Non-Fiction

Breaking Glass - Stained Glass Art and Design
> An introduction to creating stained glass art, including tools, safety, materials, design, techniques and assembly.

Shaping Stone Vol I - The Art of Soapstone Carving
> An introduction to the art of soapstone carving, including tools, safety, materials, design, techniques and finishing.

Shaping Stone Vol II - Advanced Techniques of Soapstone Carving
> Volume II picks up where Volume I ended, guiding you easily and seamlessly into the advanced tools and techniques of soapstone carving.

Zero Cost Self Publishing
> A guide on how to self publish your book, in paper and eBook formats, market internationally, collect royalties and do it all at no cost.

Zero Cost Self Publishing Series
> A series of subject specific books aimed at the various components of self publishing.

Fiction

The Marseille Scrolls
> The First Jeanne-Marie DeNord Suspense Novel
> 1st century scrolls found in 2009 in Southern France leave Jeanne-Marie in a cat and mouse game with unknown adversaries, as she hunts for answers. If she doesn't find them soon, the scrolls will be buried for another 2,000 years, and maybe Jeanne along with them.

The Exodus Scrolls
> The Second Jeanne-Marie DeNord Suspense Novel
> Jeanne finds herself in the middle of a disaster in Egypt, re-enacting the Exodus plagues. Now Jeanne is in a race to find the answer before the tenth plague kills her and half the world.

A Tapestry of Words and Demons
> A book of poetry, thoughts, images and demons, from the early years.

Songs of Words and Demons
> A book of poetry, thoughts, images and demons, from the middle years.

Demon Dreams
> A compilation of poetry.

Available in paperback and eBook formats.
www.StephenCNorton.com

About the Author

Stephen started his career as a marine biologist, subsequently spent many years managing computer support and development teams and is now a full time author, artist and publisher. He lives on the West Coast of Canada with his wife. An artist for most of his life, he's worked in many mediums, from oil painting to blown glass. For the last fifteen years he's focused on writing, publishing, carving soapstone sculptures and teaching.

He has nine books currently available in both paperback and eBook formats, including two novels, 'how-to' books on self publishing, soapstone carving and stained glass art and three poetry books. He has at least five more books planned for the next few years.

Stephen can be contacted via his personal web site, which also provides links to all sites selling his books, including CreateSpace, Amazon, Smashwords, Barnes & Noble, Apple iTunes, Kobo and other resellers, at:

www.StephenCNorton.com

Stephen is the founder and CEO of his own publishing company, Northwind Ink, which specializes in publishing and distributing soft-cover and eBooks for new authors. All his books have been self-published using the techniques described in this book. Books published by Northwind Ink include novels, memoirs, 'how-to' books and poetry. Northwind Ink's services are available at:

www.NorthwindInk.com

Disclaimer

The purpose of this book is to provide information, educate and entertain. Whilst every care has been taken in preparing the information contained in this book, neither the author nor the publisher guarantees the accuracy or currency of the content.

By using this book, you are agreeing to the following conditions:

You expressly acknowledge that neither the author nor the publisher can be held responsible for any errors or omissions and accept no liability whatsoever for any loss or damage howsoever arising from, or alleged to have been caused, directly or indirectly, by the use of this book or its contents. Use of this book and its content is entirely at your own risk.

You expressly acknowledge that all content within this book and all services provided or described within it are provided "as is", with no guarantees of completeness, accuracy or timeliness, and without representations, warranties or other contractual terms of any kind, express or implied. The author and the publisher reserve the right to remove or alter content within this book at any time without notice. All services and offerings described are subject to change without notice.

You expressly acknowledge that neither the author nor the publisher has any control over, nor responsibility for, the content or privacy practices of any Internet site listed within this book. These sites are provided to you as a convenience and the inclusion of any site link does not in any way imply endorsement by the author or the publisher.

Contents

The Zero Cost Self Publishing Series.

Publish and distribute to the world at zero cost.

This book is a part of a series of books on the art of self publishing at zero cost.

The main book is **Zero Cost Self Publishing**, available on Amazon at http://www.amazon.com/dp/1927343313. It covers the entire process from start to finish for three companies, publishing to paper and the two main eBook formats and distributing to multiple major book retailers. It provides detailed guidance for the tools required to publish, distribute and market your book.

However, some readers have requested more subject specific books, leading to the release of the *Zero Cost Self Publishing Series.* Each book of the series focuses on a single topic and sells for a price significantly lower than the main book. This allows readers to pick and choose the specific topic they need assistance with. While there is some overlap across the books in the series, each book has been carefully focused on a single specific area of the publishing process.

The book you are currently reading focuses solely on publishing using the **CreateSpace** tools and techniques. It is complete, in that you can publish your manuscript to paper, create a front and back cover, set a price, select distribution markets, sell books and receive royalties. However, it does not cover other publishing items such as eBook publishers, higher end tools for image management, linking on-line videos to your books, etc. These items are covered in detail in other books within the series. For access to the full list of books within the series please visit the **Series** web site at:

www.stephencnorton.com/home/zero-cost-publishing-series.

Introduction

The world of publishing has changed dramatically over the last ten years. In the past, publishing companies had to believe in a new author enough to risk some thousands of dollars in publishing and promoting them. If the new author worked out, the publishing company stood to make a lot more money, but if the new author didn't work out that investment was lost. Publishing a new, unknown author's first book was, and still is, a high risk proposition.

While those companies still exist, the window for success in today's fast moving environment has been steadily shrinking, meaning the risks are getting worse. The risk of publishing a new author today is much higher than it was five or ten years ago, and the potential for loss to the publishing company is a lot higher too. Sales of paper books, both hardcover and softcover, have been slowly declining over the past ten years as eBooks have been making their presence felt. Initially eBooks were a very small part of the market but over time their market share has grown.

The advent of tablets and especially smartphones with good quality screens and eBook reader software on board have suddenly made eBooks much more attractive to the general public. It's now possible to store hundreds of eBooks on your phone and read them on your way to work, or on that ten hour plane flight. Some adverts aimed at people going away for a period of time compare carrying a stack of six or ten paperbacks to loading twenty or thirty eBooks onto their phone or tablet. The comparison is obvious and the eBook option always wins.

EBooks are indeed a way of the future, though lately they seem to have reached a plateau of about thirty percent of the market. I doubt paper books will ever disappear. There's just something so physically satisfying about holding a book in your hands and turning paper pages. However the success of eBooks has introduced new companies into the publishing environment. These companies are there specifically to help you create and distribute books and a new approach to publishing has developed. The Internet has also supported the new companies as they're often much easier and more productive for the author to access and work with.

These new companies are there to help you, the author, succeed, because if you succeed, they make money. Sounds a bit odd, doesn't it? You're working so they can make money, but think it through. For them to make money the books have to sell. If the books sell then you must be making money too.

In the traditional publishing world, if you are successful, you would make five, possibly ten percent of the cover price, while the publishing house took the other ninety percent. In the new publishing environment it's almost the reverse. You can make anywhere from thirty to seventy-five percent of the cover price, while the publisher / distributor takes the remainder. That means that by helping them make money, you are receiving a much larger share of the pie. In my business career, the term 'a Win:Win solution' was very popular. It seldom worked that way, because most business relationships tend towards having a winner and a loser. However, in the new publishing environment, I do believe we are dealing with a Win:Win proposition.

Another factor which comes into play, one especially important for new authors, is that under the traditional publishing paradigm, it was, and still is, very difficult for a new author to break into the market. To succeed in the traditional world, the new author first has to win the interest of an agent, who must then catch the interest of a publishing house. Given the current economic climate and the decreasing sales potential for paper based books, it's very hard for new authors to break through.

In the new publishing environment, the on-line publishing companies provide the tools to enable the new author to publish themselves. The second key factor, possibly even more important, is that these companies provide, in addition to the publishing tools, free distribution to truly global markets.

If you do a Google search for 'self publishing companies' you'll get eleven million and more responses. Now scan through a few of those websites and see what they offer. They all have two things in common. They all claim to provide publishing and distribution services to order. But, while most claim it's free, when you get down to the fine print all of these services have a fee attached. They all want the author to pay fees to be published and they all suggest (strongly) that those large up-front costs will be recovered from the author's royalty payments at some time in the future. I don't buy that line.

Over the course of several years of searching though, I have found and now use three organizations that really do offer free self-publishing for the author. That means free from start to finish, no hidden extras, no extra fees, no completion costs, free! These three companies really do offer zero cost self-publishing, provide international distribution, and they do pay reasonable royalties.

In order for any author to take part in the new publishing environment, they need to learn which companies will work with them, what tools are available and how to make the best use of those tools.

In the *Zero Cost Self Publishing Series* of books I will introduce you to those companies and walk you through the publishing cycle for each one. Each book in the series will focus on a specific company process or functional area. I'll show you how you really can get your book published, in both paper and multiple eBook formats, distribute and sell to truly global markets and pay no up front or ongoing costs. Your books will have an excellent chance of making sales and when they do you will get royalty payments. I'll also show you additional tools and techniques for such things as cover development, graphics tools, managing images within your books and how to link to on-line videos.

The companies referenced provide the tools, support and distribution you need to succeed. I'll show you the tools that are available and teach you how to use them. At the end of each section I'll also give you an idea of how much technical ability you'll need to complete each step. Some steps are a little complex, but don't worry. If you can use a computer, you can publish your book.

After describing the tools I'll show you how to access the mechanisms that provide global distribution of your books via all the major web based sales networks, including Amazon, Apple iBooks, Barnes and Noble, Kobo and others. Best of all, the companies and tools I'll introduce you to will help you do all this, **at absolutely no cost to you.** When your book sells they will all pay you anywhere from thirty to seventy-five percent royalties, based on your cover price.

For no more than the cost of this book, I can show you how to get that first book published, distributed and selling internationally. And it doesn't stop at your first book. You can repeat the process for as many books as you can produce, all for free. Once you know the basics, the world will open up for you.

Join me, and let's start the journey to becoming a published, internationally selling author, today, at no risk and zero cost!

For other books in the series please visit the *Zero Cost Self Publishing Series* web page at:

www.stephencnorton.com/home/zero-cost-publishing-series

Publishing on CreateSpace

CreateSpace is a web based service which allows you to upload a completed electronic manuscript, publish it to soft cover paperback and distribute the title to international markets. It has no up-front costs for using the service, though it does provide in-house services at cost if you wish to use them. However, if you chose to, you can complete the publishing process entirely on your own, at zero cost.

Before going any further I'd like to mention backups. When editing your document, you may do a lot of work making a lot of changes to the document, both when you're writing it and when you're publishing the manuscript. Do not risk losing all that work.

On a regular basis, I recommend at least daily, make a backup copy of your working document. Call it *'book name copy month day'* and save it to a sub folder. You will end up with a series of copies in date sequence. That allows you to recover to yesterdays document if something catastrophic happens. You may lose a days work, but no more than that.

I also recommend making *'off-computer'* backups. Every day, or every few days, copy all your backups to another computer, network drive, USB memory plug or to a CD or DVD. That way, if the catastrophe is the complete failure of your computer, you have copies somewhere else. I use an off-computer, USB connected external drive for backups while I'm working, and then copy all my work files and the final master to a DVD when I publish the book. That is especially important if you're producing a book with lots of images in it. All your work is on a DVD so you can access everything you need if you decide to update it.

The CreateSpace process begins with your manuscript. This manuscript should be in its final form, that is, fully edited for spelling, grammar, content, continuity etc. It should also be print-ready, formatted exactly the way you wish it to be printed on the paper page. You can upload your manuscript as a .pdf, .doc, .docx, or .rtf file. PDF format is the recommended method, as it ensures that the final book will look exactly the same as the file you submitted. If you need assistance on the formatting of your manuscript and production of pdf files please refer to the book **Build Your Book Manuscript in Word at Zero Cost**, part of the Zero Cost Self Publishing Series.

In order to upload files to CreateSpace you obviously need to sign on first. Go to www.CreateSpace.com and sign up to create an account for yourself.

The expectation is that because this is your publishing site you will supply true and correct information about yourself. Name and address are especially important because that's who the cheque will be made out to and where it will be sent. By all means review CreateSpace's privacy policy before doing so, but I've never had any issues with the site.

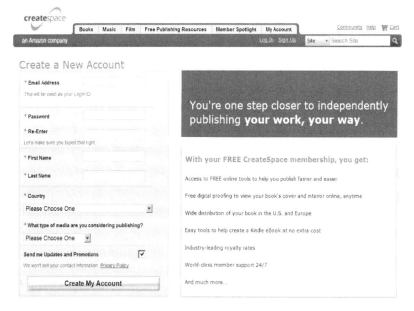

Once your account is created go to https://www.createspace.com and sign in to CreateSpace. This will bring you to your member dashboard, which provides complete management of all your projects.

This is your CreateSpace homepage. **A** is to add a new title, **B** shows your current balances across all three markets, US, UK and European. **C** lists the titles you currently have either completed or in progress. **D** shows the status of each title, 'Available' means people can buy it, 'Incomplete means it's not yet available to the public. **E** indicates the number of books that have been sold in the current month for which royalties have accumulated. **F** is the option to click on if you wish to order copies for yourself at the author production cost. **G** is the CreateSpace ID assigned to each project or book. Each book has a unique ID, used both to track the book and to provide a marketing and sales page for that specific book. **H** is the menu to access other items, including messages from CreateSpace, your royalty reports, including customized reports you can build yourself, any purchases you have made and options to edit your account settings. **I** gives you access to technical support via e-mail and telephone. In my experience the tech support has been excellent. **J** is the number of books sold this month and **K** provides a detailed breakdown of how your books are selling. All activities are started from this page.

To begin a new book simply click the *'Add New Title'* button. This will bring up the new title creation page where you name your project and decide what the project is. CreateSpace allows you to create paper books, audio CDs, MP3s, DVDs and video downloads, all of which can then be distributed to international sales sites.

Provide a title for your project and then select Paperback as your publishing option. I normally use the book title as the project title. Next, select the method you wish to use in the setup process: Guided or Expert. For your first couple of books it's probably best to use the 'Guided' process. Once you're used to the workflow you can use the single page 'Expert' option which allows you to skip around from step to step, however, in Expert mode you no longer have access to the Interior Reviewer tools, so I recommend Guided if you have pictures in your book.

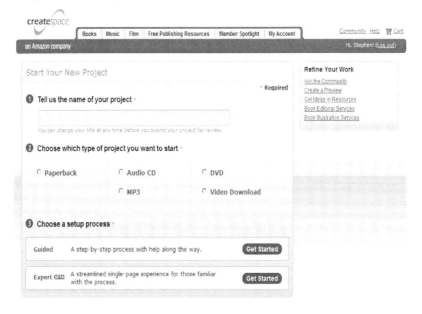

The next step is the title information. If you named your project with the title of your book then the title is already filled out. Simply double check it for spelling and capitalization. I use 'cut and paste' from the Word document master copy of my book for filling out a lot of the fields here. This ensures that the titles and subtitles I've used in the book are correctly replicated in the web pages. Enter the subtitle if your book has one. Complete the primary author field and if there are multiple authors use the *'Add Contributors'* option. If this book is part of a series fill out the series information too. For a first book, ignore the *Edition number*. Set the language. Leave the publication date blank, as the system will compete that when the book is approved for publishing. Then press the *'Save & Continue'* button. This will save the project title information and take you on to the ISBN screen. While this page is generally not changeable once saved, CreateSpace technical support can make changes to some areas, such as adding series information at a later date.

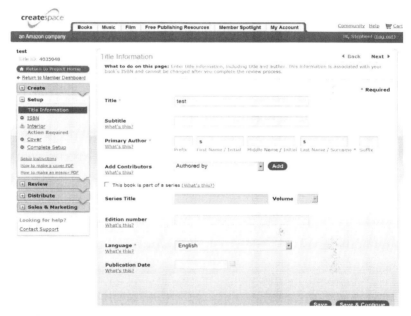

Each book you produce must have a unique International Standard Book Number (ISBN). If you have an ISBN of your own that you wish to use, select that option. If you do not have an ISBN and are only going to be publishing one or two books, then it's probably easiest simply to accept the free CreateSpace issued ISBN. This does not affect your ownership of copyright to the book in any way, it simply lists CreateSpace as the publisher. If you supply your own ISBN, you will be listed as the publisher. In order for most publishing companies to make your book available for sale on their web pages and other distribution outlets the book must have an ISBN.

This is a one-time option and cannot be changed later. Each Title and format of your book must have it's own unique ISBN. That means if you plan on creating both a paper versions and an .epub version of your book, each must have its own unique ISBN. If you choose to use your own ISBN's they must be acquired from the appropriate issuer.

In the US the main issuer is Bowker, at: http://www.bowker.com.

In Canada it is the National Library and Archives of Canada, under 'Services for Professionals', at: http://www.collectionscanada.gc.ca.

It should be noted that ISBN issue and cost varies from country to country. In the US, Bowker ISBN's cost $125 each (2014) while in Canada they are free to Canadian residents, issued in blocks of ten upon request. You are, however, required to supply one copy of your book to the National Archives at your cost, and two copies if sales exceed one hundred books. You must acquire your ISBN's from your country of residence. While Bowker offers barcodes bundled with the ISBN, they are not required for any method of book publishing covered in the Zero Cost Series.

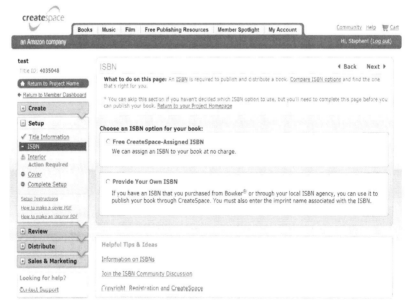

Before you decide, make sure you read the section on Channels, as using a CreateSpace ISBN does open up the Libraries and Academic sales outlets, which is not available if you use your own ISBN.

Once you've decided, click on either the *'Provide Your Own ISBN'* button or the *'Free CreateSpace Assigned ISBN'* button.

This will move us on to the interior page setup. At this point you can select the book trim size. Your first time through you will be asked to select the trim size. Later, if you do a second book, the previously selected trim size will be the default. Think of trim size as the size and shape of your book. Standard sizes offered range from 5" x 8" up to 8.5" x 11", with a variety of intermediate industry standard sizes. The 6" x 9" is a good standard size for novels, memoirs, etc. while larger sizes like 8" x 10" or 8.5" x 11" are preferably for 'how-to' books or books with a lot of color photographs or images. Go through your bookshelf or local library to get a feel for which book size would be the most appropriate for your particular book.

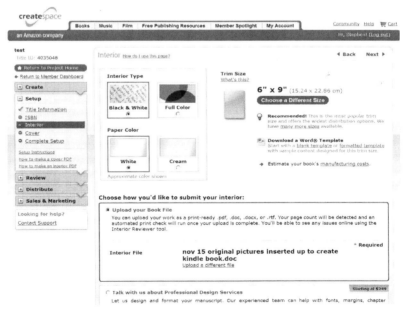

Next, choose your interior type; black and white (for text only books) or full color (for books with color photos), and the paper color you wish to use, white or cream.

For novels with no pictures, black-and-white interior type and page color of white are the usual choices. For memoirs which include photos or how-to books which include photos, the full color interior type option may be the preferred option. If using full color text, the cream paper option is greyed out. For my poetry books I used an interior type of black and white with cream paper color. This produces a book that is more aesthetically pleasing for poetry.

After selecting your paper type and color, you're ready to upload your book file. Note that if you selected the 6" x 9" option in CreateSpace, both your original Word manuscript document and the PDF document you create from it must be set to use the 6" x 9" paper size option.

Click on the *'Browse'* button and browse to the location on your computer where you stored the PDF version of your finished book. CreateSpace will accept .rtf, .doc or .docx document formats as well, but providing a PDF ensures that the page layout remains exactly the way you set it. Supplying a .doc file can allow some variation to occur during the conversion. For example, I uploaded a .doc file and the print checker reported missing 'Vivaldi' fonts which needed to be embedded in my document. I didn't use Vivaldi anywhere in my document, but somewhere in the Word document defaults, Vivaldi must have been referenced. After I re-opened my Word document and produced a .pdf file, using BullZip, the erroneous warning disappeared.

Once your file is selected you will be prompted to set the bleed, which should be the *'ends before the edge of the page'* option and select whether or not you want to run the *Interior Reviewer*. You will not get this option if you're in *'Expert'* mode. Switch back to *'Guided'* mode. The *Interior Reviewer* allows you to review online what your paper document will look like after conversion. I recommended very strongly that you use it. Scroll down and click on the *'Save'* button to begin the upload and conversion process. This will take a few minutes so be patient.

Note that there is an option shown on the webpage to talk to CreateSpace about professional interior design services, for a fee. CreateSpace provides professional assistance at all stages of the publication process, but if you're prepared to do it all yourself you can produce professional output. If you do it all yourself your production costs are zero. If you decide to use any of the offered services then obviously your production cost will not be zero.

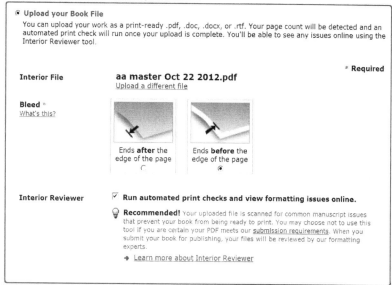

The conversion can take several minutes but once it's done the webpage will warn you if any issues were found during the automated print check and give you the option to launch the reviewer.

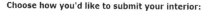

The print checker scans for gross errors in formatting and highlights any photographs with a dot-per-inch resolution of less than 200 dpi. Low resolution pictures can show grain and distortion when printed. It also checks for other issues such as margin errors, where text overlaps the allowable print areas.

Even if the automated print check didn't find any issues, click on the button to 'Launch Interior Reviewer'. The interior reviewer acts like a book reader of your actual book, displaying it as it will look when printed on paper. It allows you to review your document, either as a page by page display or as an overall view of all pages at once. Review both the overall and the page by page displays, looking for any discrepancies or issues.

Because of the different display method, errors which may not have been visible in the Word or PDF versions can show up at this stage. Incorrect use of 'Section Break, Odd or Even page' are most easily seen here. Be aware that this is the most accurate display, as it replicates exactly what the book will look like. The previous displays you've used when viewing both Word and PDF file formats are only approximate displays of the final layout. If your book looked fine in the previous displays, but looks wrong in this display, this display should be taken as the more reliable.

On the page by page displays there is a dashed box around the edge of each page. Anything extending beyond the dashed box is an error as this will not print correctly on the book. Return to your Word document and correct the margin issues.

Notice that the first page of your book interior is displayed in 'real book' format, on the right-hand side of the book, exactly as if you had opened the book to the title page. Any errors reported by the system are listed on the right, highlighted by red stars.

Switch to the overall display (below). You notice immediately that some of the pages have red stars beside them.

This indicates that there is at least one error on that page. Explanations of the error are listed to the right of the display. Double click on the error pages to switch the reviewer back to the side-by-side view and display those specific pages. They should be reviewed in detail to see what caused the problem and correct the issue.

If a page has a red star, click on the page, which will switch the display to side-by-side pages. The red star will now point to the error on the page. Click on the red star to see a detailed explanation of the error. Fix the error in your original word document.

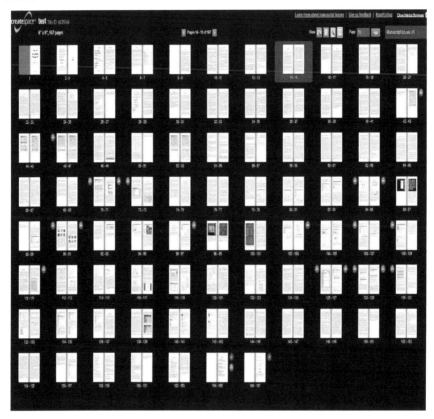

In some cases you may be prepared to accept the warning. For example, if the picture is less than two hundred dots per inch (dpi), but it's the only copy of the picture that you have, you have no choice but to use the low resolution picture. You can use a graphics tool such as the FastStone Viewer (http://faststone.org) to increase the dpi, however, increasing dpi reduces the picture size. Maintaining the size while increasing the dpi interpolates the missing details, so the result may not be any improvement over the original low resolution image.

Once the identified errors are reviewed, switch to the page by page display, start at the beginning of the book and review it from start to finish, page by page, in detail.

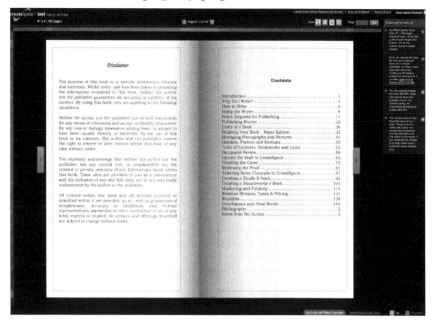

As you go through the rest of the book look for anything 'different'. This could be extra blank space where there shouldn't be any, titles that don't always fall the same distance down the page. In some books that may not be easily noticeable. In others, like my poetry books, where almost every page has a title, it's disconcerting to the reader to have titles bouncing up and down the page by a line or two. Make sure titles are always the same distance down the page. Careful use of style management and adding point spacing before and after the text on the chapter heading style should address this problem. (See '**Build Your Book Manuscript**' in the Zero Cost Series.) Check that your selected fonts came through properly. If not, read up on Word's help files for embedding fonts in the document, or check the PDF writer to ensure it contains the fonts. If your selected fonts don't come through properly after two or three attempts, consider changing the font. Always check for spelling, correct word usage and grammar.

If you find any errors, like the margin issue below, now is the time to correct them. This display shows that my Bibliography page has it's margins set too far to the left, and thus some of my text will not be printed. This was probably caused by a *'Cut & Paste'* which brought in formatting information from the separate Bibliography file. Return to the original manuscript document. Repeat the paste using *'Paste Special, Unformatted Text'* or simply adjust the margins on this one page in the master document.

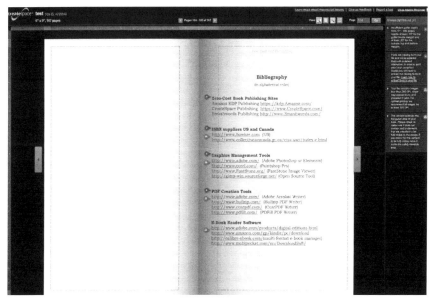

If errors are found you must always go back to your original word processor document, fix the error, re-print to pdf and check on the pdf file. If everything looks good in pdf, re-upload the file to CreateSpace and then re-check with the On-line Reviewer tool.

Once you've completed your review and you're happy with the book within the on-line reviewer, click on the 'Save & Continue' button. If you're not happy or found errors, go back to your original document and update it. Once everything looks good, move on to the book cover.

Technical Complexity: low

Filling out web forms, editing Word docs, creating pdf files, uploading files to a web, reviewing text layouts.

Creating the Cover

From the Cover homepage you have four choices. First, decide if you want the cover to be Matte or Glossy. I use both, depending on the type of book I'm producing, but most commercial publishing houses use glossy covers so let's go with that for the first book.

Next you have to decide whether to build your own cover online, use CreateSpace's professional design group, for which there is a fee, or upload a print ready PDF cover you have created.

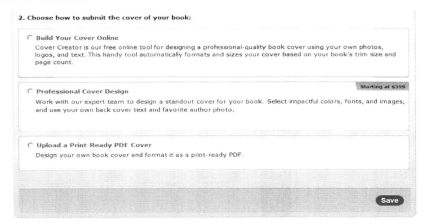

I found that uploading the print ready PDF cover is a bit painful because you have to manually calculate and adjust the book spine width depending on how many pages are in your book. This means if you've built your cover and then for some reason you add a section to the book, add more pages or remove a section, you must rebuild your PDF cover with a recalculated spine width. I've never used this method.

I've never used any of the professional services offered either, so can't provide any comments on the quality or usefulness of the services. However, our goal here is zero-cost, so we're going to do this step ourselves. I use the *'Build Your Cover Online'* option, so let's select that option, and then go ahead and click on the *'Launch Cover Creator'* button.

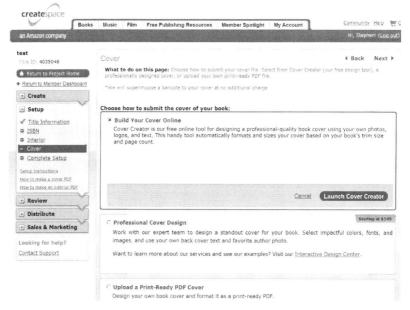

This will create a workspace, open the cover designer and present the first option: cover style. All cover designs are initially presented as 'Spineless'. This simply means that the template does not yet have a book spine width configured. This is done automatically by the system, based on the number of pages in the book.

The Hawthorn 6 x 9

The Hickory 6 x 9

The Juniper 6 x 9

The Magnolia 6 x 9

The Mangrove 6 x 9

The Maple 6 x 9

All of the supplied designs come with a default color scheme of matching background and font colors, but within the scheme you have some ability to change those colors. You also have the ability to use one of the default styles but still embed one of your own photographs into that style.

All the supplied options come with some areas blanked out, indicated by the white boxes in the examples above. These are reserved for things like the authors photo, your own publishing logo if you have provided your own ISBN, and a reserved space for the ISBN and barcode which will go on the back cover. Barcodes are required in order to sell the book via most international booksellers. Regardless of whether you choose to supply your own ISBN or use CreateSpace's ISBN, the barcode is always supplied by CreateSpace at no charge.

Some of the possible cover designs are shown above and below. Note that not all covers have all the blank boxes. Some allow for only the ISBN / barcode, some for the ISBN / barcode and author photo and some for ISBN / barcode, author photo and your own publishers logo. If you select a cover style with all three blanks, but only wish to use one or two, just leave that data field blank. However, if you pick a style which does not have the blank you want, you can't add it in. In that case, you'd have to create your cover from scratch.

| The Chestnut 6 x 9 | The Cottonwood 6 x 9 | The Cypress 6 x 9 |
| The Elm 6 x 9 | The Fir 6 x 9 | The Ginkgo 6 x 9 |

At this point you need to select a cover design. CreateSpace provides five pages worth of cover designs, so go through them carefully one by one and select the one that you like best. All of the options with pictures allow you to upload your own photograph or use one from the CreateSpace library. My preferred cover is the Palm on page 4 as it allows me to provide my own custom built front and back covers. This option adjusts the spine width appropriately as the number of pages in the book interior changes, so I don't have to worry about that.

For this book I'm going to start with The Elm, an option which doesn't have pictures. However because I selected this option doesn't mean I can't come back later, change my mind and select something else. Most of the fields that I complete for my first cover will carry over cleanly to another cover design. While I like the layout of the Elm, I'm not that enthusiastic about the orange default color so the first thing I'll do is change the color.

Go ahead and select the cover design that you prefer.

Within each design you have sub-options, called themes, which allow you to change the font styles, colors and background pictures. Themes allow you a limited amount of control over the font style and size. Other options give some control over font and background color.

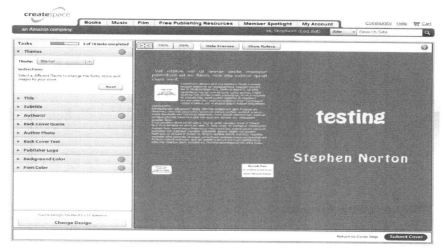

Different designs and theme combinations have different options, colors, fonts and text boxes, all of which you can modify to some extent. However, you do not have the ability to select the font of your choice from a large array of fonts, so a given design may be good, but you may not be able to get the font 'look' that you want.

The Mulberry 6 x 9   The Oak 6 x 9   The Pagoda 6 x 9

The Palm 6 x 9   The Pine 6 x 9   The Poplar 6 x 9

After doing some work on the Elm, changing colors, fonts and titles, I came to the conclusion that I couldn't make the Elm do what I wanted to do (mostly because of fonts and colors). So I switched back to my preferred standard, The Palm, which is the option that allows me to upload my own custom-designed front and back cover pages. However, because I do like the layout of the Elm cover, I'll replicate it in my graphics tool and simply use the fonts that I prefer. The Palm allows me to upload separate front and back covers and let the system calculate the spine width. The Pine option requires you to upload the complete front, back and spine as a combined, single jpeg file, which means calculating your own spine width. I find it easier to simply use the Palm and let the system calculate the spine width for me.

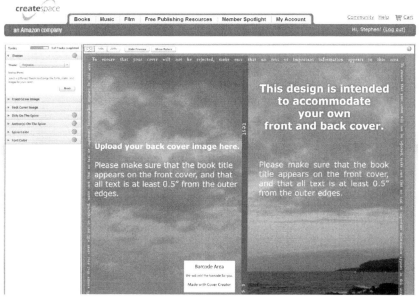

A full front cover for a 6" x 9" book should be a JPEG image file, 6.25" by 9.5" with a resolution of at least 400 dpi. I normally create my cover pages at 600 dpi. If you use other book sizes or book cover styles, be sure to check the CreateSpace instructions for the size that your cover page or partial page JPEG should be.

Using either of the options that require you to create your own cover from scratch does mean you need a graphics tool, something like Paint Shop Pro, Adobe Elements/Photoshop or the open source tool GIMP. If you don't have a tool like that and don't want to spend the money because you're only going to do one book, the easiest thing to do is use one of CreateSpace's provided cover pages. Most still allow you to upload your own photo into the appropriate spot on the cover, or use one of the CreateSpace provided images. The free tool FastStone will allow you to do some image manipulation, like re-sizing, but is not really intended for full image creation. Any of these options enable you to create a professional looking cover without having to spend any money, nor do you need to spend a great deal of time and effort learning a graphics tool. For more information on using full graphics tools please see the Series listing for **Book Cover Creation at Zero Cost**.

(www.stephencnorton.com/home/zero-cost-publishing-series)

Obviously you won't create your book all in one sitting. You'll do a part and then come back later on to complete the next step. Simply clicking on the project title from your Dashboard will bring you to the overview page as shown below. This clearly indicates those areas that you've completed (green ticks) and those items which must still be dealt with (red circles).

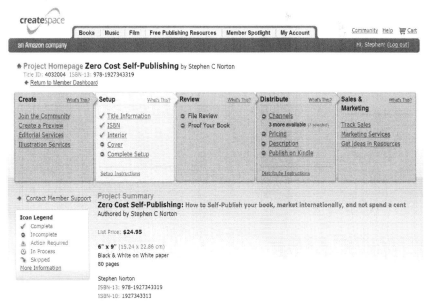

While the book is in progress I find it easiest to use this page, as it provides me direct access to any stage of the publishing process. As you can see from the screen print above, I have completed the Title, ISBN and Interior steps, but my 'Cover' and 'Completing setup' have red circles beside them, indicating that those items are not yet completed. Selecting the 'Cover' option opens the 'Edit Cover' screen.

As I've already done some work on my cover I now have the option of continuing to edit my work to date, or starting over again using a different design. I'll continue editing. Note that the work I've done so far is displayed as a thumbnail image. It's worth noting that we can re-start our work at any stage, at any time during the publishing process, uploading a completely new interior file, re-starting the cover from scratch, selecting a different design, even changing the size of our book. You will get a warning that previous work will be lost, but you always have the option of beginning again if you're not satisfied with what you've done so far. You can always step back and re-start your project. The one exception is the ISBN. Once assigned to a book, the ISBN is permanently committed to that particular project.

Click on 'Edit Cover' to continue working on the cover. This will take you into the cover creation and edit screen.

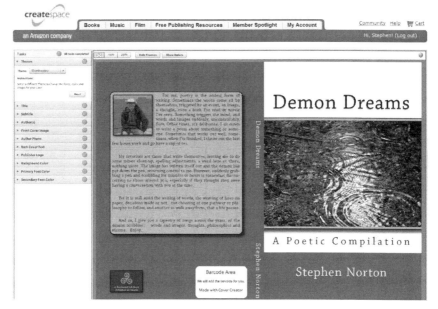

For my book 'Demon Dreams' I used a CreateSpace formatted cover and uploaded the picture from my own library. First I selected the layout, in this case, 'The Oak'.

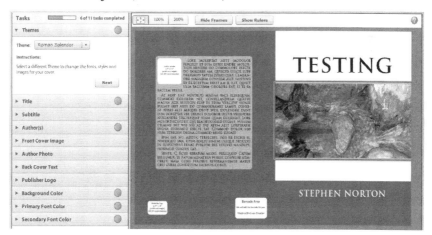

Notice that this pre-formatted cover has spaces reserved for Author Photo and Publisher Logo, and the back cover blurb is formatted inside a box.

A second layout / design control is the Theme, a drop down menu giving several alternative options to the basic design. Click on the *'Theme'* drop-down and click on each theme to see what affect the change has on the display. I decided to switch the initial theme of Roman Elegance to ShadowPlay, as I preferred the look of the text.

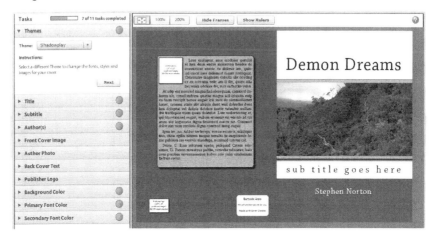

Next, click on Title to enter the title and subtitle to enter that if you have one.

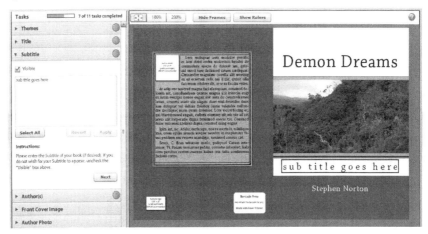

Notice that the Subtitle field has an option for *'Visible'*. Unticking this box changes the box to *'Invisible'* and removes the sub title from the cover.

Click on Author to enter the authors name, then click on Front Cover Image to select an image for the cover. This can be one of your own, or one from the CreateSpace Gallery.

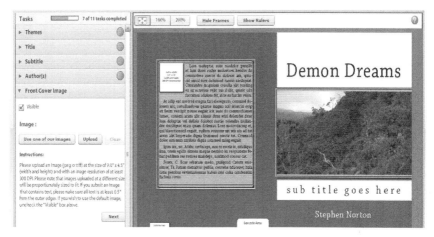

If you're going to use your own picture, read the size and format information, use a tool like FastStone to adjust your picture to meet the requirements and then upload the picture to your cover workspace. If you want to use an image from the gallery, click on the *'Use one of our images'* button. This will take you into the Art Gallery.

You can browse the galleries, reviewing the various images to find one which suits your book cover.

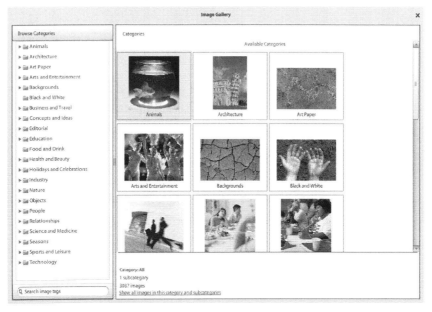

Click on any image to get a slightly bigger image and the option to select it for your cover.

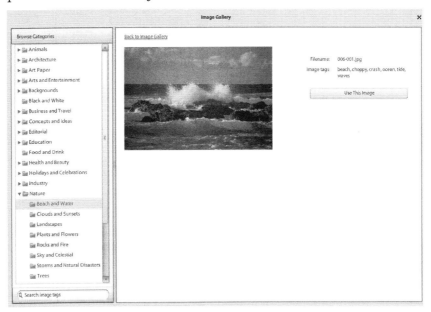

Click *'Use This Image'* to have the image imported into your cover.

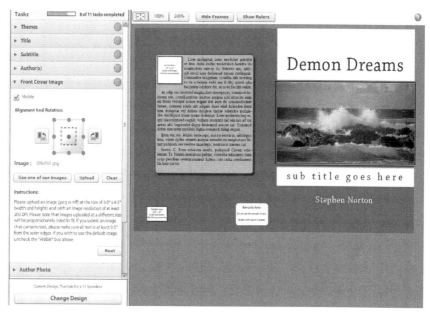

Carry on with the teasks listed on the menu to the left. Change colors to suit, enter back cover text, etc.

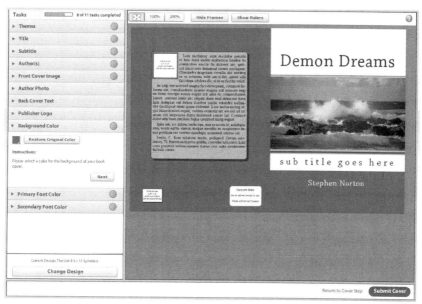

If you have an authors photo and / or company logo you can upload those images. If not, un-tick the 'Visible' box to remove them from the cover. On the display below the author's photo is invisible. The location of the logo is outlined as I've just made it invisible. Once I move on to the next task the black outline box will disappear.

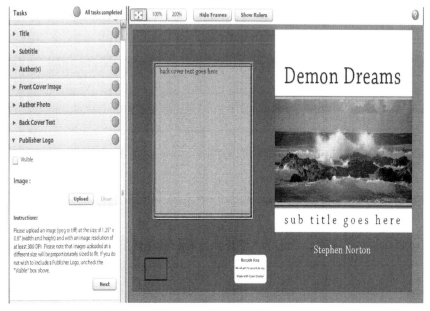

From the cover editor you can continue working on the cover until it's completed. Once finished, click on the 'Submit Cover' which will build the cover, create a thumbnail image and return you to the 'Edit Cover' screen. From there, click on the 'Complete Cover' button to submit the cover for final processing.

There is a copyright issue related to cover photos. In order for you to publish your book, you must own copyright to everything in the book, or have written permission from the owner allowing you to use it. This applies to text and photos in the book interior but it also applies to the art used on both front and back covers. If you took the photographs then you own the copyright. If you found the art on an Internet web page, then you need permission from the artist to use it, unless the site clearly states the contents are public domain or free for use. Just because it's posted on the web doesn't mean its available for free commercial use on your book.

Once all the steps are completed, and you've reviewed your interior and cover, completed all error corrections and are ready to call the book 'finished' select the option from the side menu to *'Complete Setup'*. This will bring up the screen where you submit your completed files to CreateSpace for review. Click on the *'Submit Files for Review'* button.

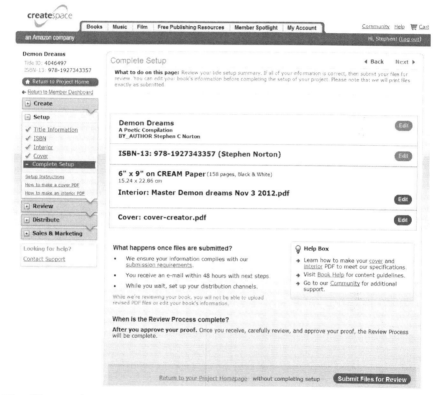

You'll get the message screen below and your book files will be frozen until after the review is completed. Your book isn't published yet, but we're getting close.

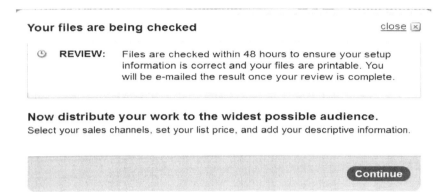

Once confirmed by CreateSpace, you will then be able to order a proof copy of your book and use the online proofing tools to review what your book will look like when printed.

You can still make changes after completing the setup, so if your 'Proof' has flaws you can submit a new interior file or re-edit your cover pages. You will be warned that information may be lost when returning to the earlier screens but this really means you'll have to re-submit files for re-build, so most of the work done on the cover page will still be there, you'll just have to repeat some steps on re-submission.

While you're waiting for the submission to be reviewed and approved, you can fill out the description fields of your book and set sales channels and pricing.

Technical Complexity: low to high

If using CreateSpace supplied cover designs complexity is low, mostly filling out web screen fields and uploading files.

If creating your own cover from scratch, complexity can range from low to high, depending on the complexity of your graphic designs and your familiarity with the tools. See *Cover Creation* in the Zero Cost Series.

Selecting Sales Channels and Markets

Select the '*Distribute*' option from the Main Menu list on the left of the screen. This provides access to select the sales channels you wish to use, the price you want to assign to the book, create or modify your book description and optionally transfer your files to the Amazon KDP site to begin the process to publish it as a Kindle eBook. Click on Channels to display the Channels screen. To select or de-select a channel, click on the arrow beside the channel name.

Within the Standard Distribution environment you have the option of the first three channels:

- Amazon.com
- Amazon Europe
- CreateSpace eStore

You can pick all three or none of these. For example if you have written a memoir which you only want to distribute yourself and not make use of any of the web sales outlets whatsoever, you wouldn't select any of the channels. You would simply order books for your own consumption at the wholesale author price. If you're writing for the international market you would select all three.

While Amazon.com basically covers the US, it is accessible for anywhere in the world, selling books in US dollars. Amazon Europe covers the United Kingdom (Amazon.co.uk), selling in pounds and European countries, selling in euros. The Europe option distributes to Amazon sites in several countries, including Germany (Amazon.de), France (Amazon.fr) Italy (Amazon.it), Spain, etc. While the pricing on all European sites is in euros, the language of the site changes to match the country designator. This may not help English writers but if you have access to translation capabilities this could mean additional sales potential as you could publish additional alternate language versions.

Expanded Distribution, which at one time had a cost attached, is now free. It makes your book available to other commercial outlets such as Barnes & Noble, but because there are more sellers involved the percentage royalty paid to you drops by about 60%. For example, a book which pays an $8 royalty when sold via the Amazon market drops to $3 when sold through expanded distribution. However, it does increase your market coverage.

In order to access the Libraries and Academic Institutions outlets you <u>must</u> use an ISBN number supplied by CreateSpace. You cannot use your own number. I have never made use of this option as I prefer to provide my own ISBN's. If you want to access libraries at no cost, use an ISBN as offered by CreateSpace or use the Smashwords eBook publishing service, which is also covered in the Zero Cost Series of books.

Regardless of which sales channels you've selected, you need to set the retail cover price for the book. This is done through the pricing panel.

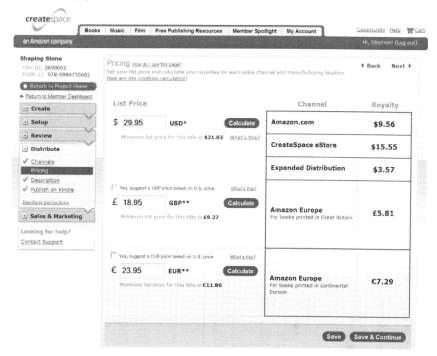

All pricing is set initially in US dollars (USD). When you set the price the royalty field is automatically filled in for each of the other channels. If you selected Amazon Europe you also have the option to set prices for United Kingdom Pounds (£) and European Euros (€). To make your life easy CreateSpace automatically calculates those prices based on your US dollar price, however you can manually override those and set your own international pricing if you prefer. Notice that this book is one for which I used the Expanded Distribution and notice the royalty paid on the Expanded Distribution. Also note the difference between the CreateSpace royalty and the Amazon royalty. Obviously it's preferable to sell your book directly from the CreateSpace web site, however Amazon has a much wider distribution outlet and is much more recognized among the general populace. Amazon may also offer a better shipping cost to purchasers than CreateSpace, especially for cross border shipping where duties may be incurred depending on price of the book. This is obviously a benefit to your readers but at a reduced royalty to you.

Unless you wish to keep your book private and personal I would certainly recommend selecting all three of the main distribution outlets. The Expanded Distribution may or may not be useful to you. Does a sale on Barnes & Noble add to your revenue, or take away a sale which would otherwise occur on Amazon? That's a question I have been unable to answer.

Next, click on the *'Description'* option in the menu and fill out the description fields for your book. You are allowed up to four thousand characters for the description. That count includes all spaces, punctuation and paragraph breaks. You will want to spend some time and effort on developing this description. Compressing your fifty thousand word book into a clear and concise description within four thousand characters can be a writing task unto itself. Four thousand characters is roughly seven hundred words. (Word will display character and word counts under *'File, Properties, Statistics'.*)

Developing this description and making it attractive and interesting is critical for promoting your book. It's the only information the potential buyer will have to review your book, other than the cover image.

The next task is to select the BISAC Category for your book. This is a standardized set of book categories created by the international Book Industry Systems Advisory Committee, used to help describe books on a common basis. Click on the *'Choose'* button to select from the drop down menus. Spend some time here going through the various categories that may describe your book and pick the one that best describes your book. Some people browse for books by category, rather than searching by title or author name. It can be useful to look at similar books on Amazon and see what other authors are using for a BISAC category code, though not everyone reports a code. Amazon creates sub categories based on the BISAC selected, and assigns ratings based on the number of books sold in that category. It's always better to be rated number 50 in a category of 500, than to be rated as number 5,000,000 in the basic category of Books.

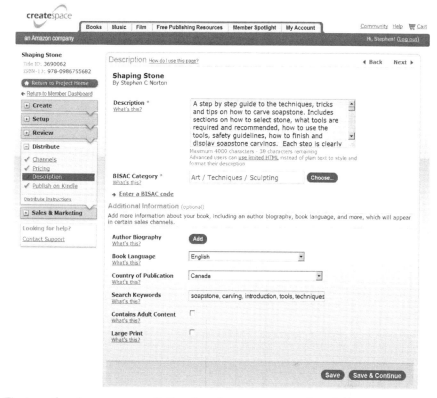

Enter the language of the book, country of publication (your country, not CreateSpace's country) appropriate key words to support purchasers keyword searches and whether the book contains adult content or is in Large Print.

Now you've selected your sales channels and set your pricing the book is ready to be posted for sale, as soon as you accept the proof of the book. CreateSpace provides a sales page for your book directly from CreateSpace, and if you selected the additional sales channels these web pages will become available within a few days, usually around 5 to 7 business days after you approve the book.

The CreateSpace web site for your book is the CreateSpace site address plus your book ID. For example the CreateSpace sale page for my first novel, '**The Marseille Scrolls**' is:

http://www.CreateSpace.com/3642987

3642987 is the code assigned to my book by CreateSpace.

Amazon follows the same general format, and thus the sales page for my book **'Breaking Glass, An Introduction to Stained Glass Art & Design'**, on Amazon is:

http://www.amazon.com/dp/1927343089

1927343089 is the code assigned to my book by Amazon.

Both CreateSpace and Amazon create sales pages for your book. The CreateSpace sales page is shown below, followed by the Amazon sales page.

Amazon also provides the author with an Author's Page where you can post your author picture, profile and biography and collect all your Amazon published books into a single location. This requires you to set up an Amazon account as well, which you will need to do if / when you decide to create a Kindle version of your book. The Amazon Author pages are covered in more detail in the Zero Cost Series book on **Publishing to Amazon KDP**.

The CreateSpace page provides all the book information, size, color, number of pages, categories, etc, and displays the full 4,000 character description. Purchasers can be directed to this page and can purchase your book by adding it to the cart and supplying shipping and billing information. This page charges the full cover price you designated, so you, as the author, should not purchase copies for yourself from here. For buying your own copies, go to your dashboard and click on the *'Order Copies'* option to the right of the book title. The dashboard route will allow you to order copies for yourself at the manufacturers production cost rather than the retail cover price.

Breaking Glass 🔲 Like < 0

Stained Glass Art and Design
Authored by Stephen C Norton

Welcome to Breaking Glass, an introduction to the art and design of stained glass. A step by step guide to the techniques, tricks and tips on how to create Stained Glass Art, 'Breaking Glass' includes sections on selecting glass, the tools which are required and others which are recommended. Subjects covered include how to use those tools, safety guidelines, how to cut, grind, fit and assemble the pieces and display beautiful stained glass art. Each step is clearly explained via text, photographs and on-line videos.

~
Today, stained glass remains both an industry and a hobby. Churches still order stained glass windows for their cathedrals, mostly as depictions of scenes from the bible. Many commercial buildings have stained glass art prominently displayed. People buy stained glass 'Tiffany' style lamps for their living rooms and order colorful windows for their homes, ranging from scenery to abstract art. A good quality lamp can cost hundreds of dollars. Stained glass windows can easily go into the thousands.

List Price: $29.95

[Add to Cart]

Continue Shopping

As with any art, you can buy something created by someone else, or you can learn the art and do it yourself. Unlike some art forms, stained glass can be done in small scale by anyone with an interest and a steady hand. Pre-done patterns can be purchased at the local bookstore. Most cities have a glass shop which carries glass and stained glass supplies. If not, Internet sites abound. Tools are relatively inexpensive and easy to acquire. All you need is a little assistance, a guide to walk you through the steps of creation. What you have in your hands is that guide.

'Breaking Glass' is written to give you the introductory guide to creating stained glass art, including lampshades, windows and three dimensional objects. It introduces you to the various tools and techniques used, then walks you through the five steps of creating, cutting, grinding, assembly and finishing. Following along with the book allows the you to understand the art form, including creation of your own patterns. By the end, you will be able to tailor-make your own stained glass art.

I've chosen to make this book pictorial rather than wordy. I'm a firm believer that a picture speaks a thousand words, so I've tried to show, and only talked enough to guide you through what the picture depicts. I've also chosen the size of the book so I can fit in lots of pictures, while keeping the pictures big enough that you can clearly see the detail shown without needing a magnifying glass. At various key spots I also provide links to on-line videos, providing greater detail on techniques. Lastly, I've focused on giving you an overall introduction to creating stained glass art, so you can create your own designs and art to suit your needs.

You don't have to be an expert to follow the steps in this book. You don't have to have any experience in glass work, you simply need to have an interest and a desire to create something. I will guide you through the process in five easy-to-follow steps. You only need a few tools, though I show you other tools that can be useful. You can choose how much to invest and how many tools to buy. The basic tools can be purchased for one hundred to one hundred and fifty dollars. The glass is easy to buy and inexpensive, ranging anywhere from five to ten dollars per square foot.

Sound interesting? Well, if you haven't already done so, buy the book. Pick up a few tools, buy some glass, follow along with the book and let's start breaking glass.

Publication Date:	May 21 2012
ISBN/EAN13:	1927343089 / 9781927343081
Page Count:	114
Binding Type:	US Trade Paper
Trim Size:	8.5" x 11"
Language:	English
Color:	Full Color
Related Categories:	Crafts & Hobbies / Glass & Glassware

If you've selected Amazon as one of your sales channels, CreateSpace passes the information on your book to Amazon for display on the Amazon Books webpage.

Notice that the Amazon web page also displays the 4,000 character description. On the Amazon page, clicking on the authors name will offer options to search for additional books by this author, or go to their author page.

We've completed all the ancillary information, and by now your book submission review should have completed, so let's go take a look at our 'proof' copy.

Technical Complexity: low to high

Low for filling out web forms, potentially high for creating the 4,000 character description of your book.

Reviewing the Proof

Once you have submitted your book to CreateSpace your files will be reviewed to ensure they meet CreateSpace's requirements. If they do, you'll receive an email stating:

Congratulations your files are printable!

We've reviewed the interior and cover files for Your Book Title, #1234567 and they meet submission requirements.

The next step in the publishing process is to proof your book:

Now you can review the proof copy. As mentioned earlier, this can be done online, in which case there is no cost. However, as this is your first book, I do recommend spending the money to get a paper proof copy. Once you're familiar with the quality that CreateSpace produces, you can do it all on-line at no cost.

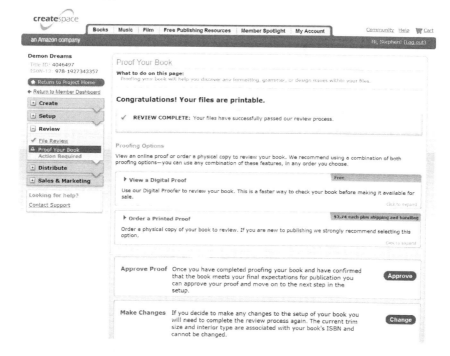

Ordering a single 'proof' copy of your book from CreateSpace is quite in-expensive. A 250 page black and white 6" x 9" book will cost less than $5.00, and shipping is reasonable: around $7 to Canada, around $4 for most of the US. A full color book will cost more than a black and white book, but books are sold to the author 'at cost', so unless you have a 500 page full-color book the costs are quite reasonable. A 180 page 6" x 9" with full color photos every few pages costs $13.45 (2014). Having said that, definitely use the free on-line 'View a Digital Proof' tool **before** ordering a paper copy. You may find issues that you can correct before paying for the paper copy. Buying the paper copy at standard shipping rates also takes two to three weeks for delivery. To review the final proof on-line, click on *View a Digital Proof*.

Like the Online Reviewer tool, the Online Digital Proofer tool is excellent, allowing you to view your book by full front and back cover, page by page and as a multipage display as shown below. It's basically the same tool as the Interior Reviewer, but adds the cover pages to your review. You also have the option of downloading a PDF of your completed book. By all means do that as well, for your own off-line reviewing, but I prefer to use the on-line tool as I believe it gives a more book-like view of the files. Click on *Launch Digital Proofer* to review your book proof on-line.

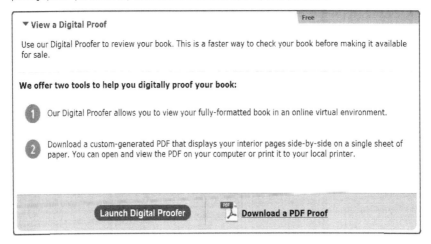

Proofing Options

View an online proof or order a physical copy to review your book. We recommend using a combination of both proofing options—you can use any combination of these features, in any order you choose.

▼ View a Digital Proof   Free

Use our Digital Proofer to review your book. This is a faster way to check your book before making it available for sale.

We offer two tools to help you digitally proof your book:

1 Our Digital Proofer allows you to view your fully-formatted book in an online virtual environment.

2 Download a custom-generated PDF that displays your interior pages side-by-side on a single sheet of paper. You can open and view the PDF on your computer or print it to your local printer.

Launch Digital Proofer   Download a PDF Proof

The first screen displays the book's cover, back and front.

Check the picture and text alignments of the covers, the wording of the 'blurbs', make sure the text is easily readable and that there is no overlap on the reserved boxes such as the UPC code box.

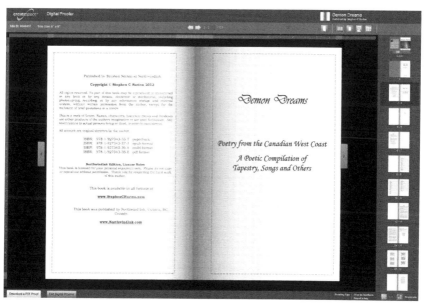

The next pages displayed are the first interior pages. As we did when we reviewed our book in Word and the Interior Reviewer, I recommend using both page by page and multipage displays. At this point I will check the first few pages, and then switch to the multi-page view.

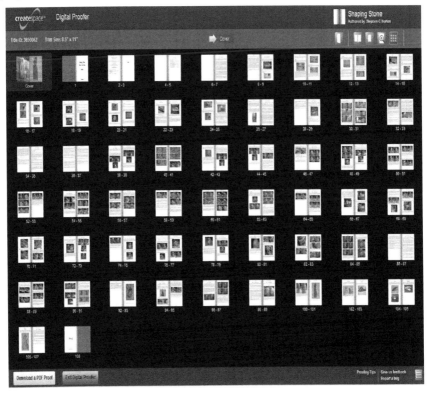

The multipage display allows you to overview the book and see if any of your pages look odd or asymmetrical. This is very important for books such as the one displayed above where I have a lot of text wrapped around a lot of pictures.

Notice that on the example screen below, while there are no warning icons, I can easily see that the images are not all on the same side of the page as I'd intended. This is most likely due to issues with section and page breaks in the Word document. The Digital Proofer allows you to double check the 'printed' version, to ensure that what you think is on the left page of your book, really is on the left side.

On this display it's obvious that something has gone wrong with my desired page layout. I wanted all the pictures on the left side of the book, but one of my section / page breaks was incorrect and some of the images ended up on the right hand side of the book. This should have been caught during the interior page review, but for whatever reason it wasn't. This means I must now go back to my original Word document, make adjustments, print to PDF, review the page layout in the PDF file and then upload the interior file to CreateSpace again. Uploading a new interior will force me to re-open my cover. In this case I simply need to open my cover for editing, then save the unchanged cover again. This forces the cover creator to re-calculate the spine width for the new interior, because my interior change may have changed the number of pages in the book. Now I need to re-submit all my files for review again, which will bring me back to this step, final proofing.

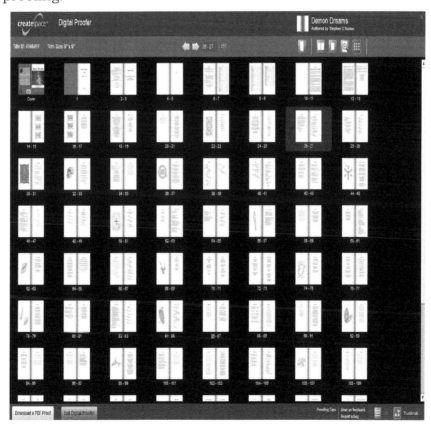

Even the book displayed below, an all text novel, benefits from the multipage review as you can see which pages look different from the others. Any differences or large blank spots should be investigated. While errors or oddities in page coverage should have been caught during the earlier interior review, it is not unusual to discover something you want to change even at this late date. Don't let it bother you if you find something you need or want to change. It's best to catch and correct things here, before you commit the book to being published and made available to readers. It seems that no matter how many times I have others edit-check my books, every time I pick one up and read through it I see something I'd like to adjust, just to make it a little bit better. However, you do need to stop somewhere and actually print the book and release it for publishing and distribution. Even commercially produced books using the traditional method are subject to occasional errors.

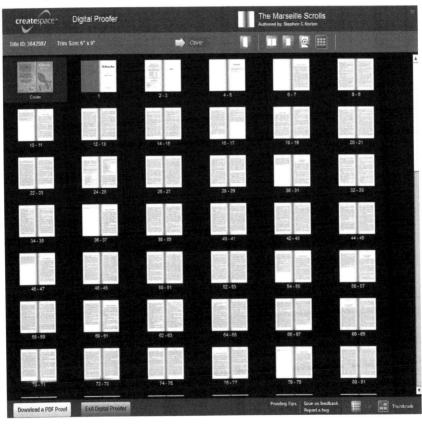

After any re-submission of your files, you should repeat the entire process of proofing your book. Check the cover again. Check the interior using the multi-page display again. Then select the page by page display for a detailed review of placement of text and pictures on each page.

Read through the entire book, page by page, checking for any errors. Are chapter headings aligned properly? Is the text aligned on the page correctly? Are headers and footers correct and on the right pages? Are page numbers where you wanted them to be, on the right pages, and numbered sequentially and correctly? Again, check spelling and grammar, word use, etc. The online proofing tool provides an option to download a PDF of your finalized document and I recommend doing this and double checking things yet again.

Yes, you did all this on the Word document before you uploaded it, and you did it again on the interior reviewer after the upload. Now do it again. I know I've recommended double checking everything a lot of times, but it's very easy to overlook an error and the more times you check the more errors you will catch, and thus the more professional your end result will be. Murphy's Law says you will always find another thing to correct or change, no matter how many times you've checked before.

There's nothing worse than getting your hands on the first copy of your just-released-for-sale book and immediately finding an obvious error on page four. My first novel had 'comment sa va' on page one. My French said it was correct plus I'd checked it using the on-line translators and they said it was fine, but the first three buyers all said it should have been 'comment ca va'. Turned out to be my Quebecois French (sa) versus Parisian French (ca), but everyone was much happier with 'comment ca va'. So I quickly edited my master document, changed it and re-released the book as fast as I could.

One of the huge advantages of this new paradigm of publishing is that such errors can be corrected quickly and painlessly. There is no large run of books which must be destroyed and re-printed to correct the error. Nor is there any cost to updating the books content. You simply correct the electronic master at CreateSpace, run through the review and approval process again and the next book ordered contains the updated and / or corrected version.

Once you are finally satisfied that the document has been as proofed as you can possibly make it, go back into the Review screen and either order a paper proof (recommended), or click the button to 'Approve' the proof based on just your digital review.

If this is your first book I strongly recommend you order a paper copy of the proof and review that before approving the book for release. I've found that reviewing a paper proof is a totally different experience to reviewing an on-line proof. It has a different look and feel, and for some reason you see things in the paper proof which were not apparent in the on-line proof. The two to three week shipping time also allows your mind to relax and forget the details of what you meant to say. That means when you read the paper proof you're much more likely to read the words that are actually written on the page, rather than what you think you wrote. You can also mark up the paper copy with a red or green pen, which again, for some reason, makes it easier to catch errors in wording, content continuity and narrative flow. Once you've reviewed the paper proof in detail and corrected all issues found, re-submit the document as a new interior, go through the review process again and come back to this screen to approve the proof. (Hah! Finally!)

You have all the same options, digital on-line review, order a paper proof copy, make further changes or Approve the document for publishing.

Click on the 'Approve' button.

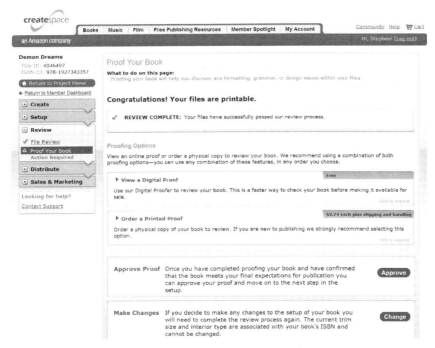

You'll be prompted one more time to confirm that you approve the book for publishing.

Confirm Approval

Please confirm that you have completed proofing your book and that the book meets your final expectations for publication. Once you approve your proof it will become available for sale in the channels that you have selected.

Cancel **Approve**

This moment can be both exhilarating and terrifying. You're about to publish your creation for the first time and make it available to the world. Pressing the button has the potential to change your world, and the world's view of you. It's a truly unique first book moment. Savor it!

Go ahead and click on the *'Approve'* button to confirm that you approve the proof.

With the proof authorized, either from a paper copy or just the online proofing tool, your CreateSpace paperback book is now complete. It's available for sale on CreateSpace it and will be available for sale on the other sales channels you selected within a few days.

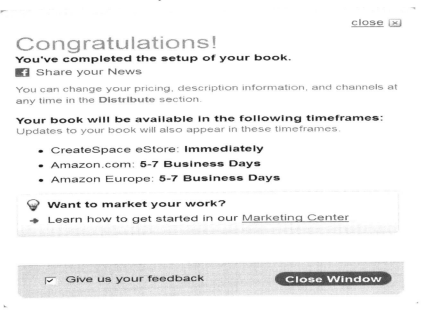

Technical Complexity: low

Filling out web forms and viewing web browser displays, reading and editing your paperback proof, correcting word documents.

Accounts, Taxes and ITIN's

Having published the book, the next thing to deal with is tracking sales and getting paid. On the left hand menu list is a section titled '*My Account*'. This covers the message center, reports, your own purchases and account settings. The message center displays messages from CreateSpace on the status of your book during publication and any purchases. You will also get copies of those email forwarded to the email address you register in your account settings. Click on '*Edit Account Settings*' to access this information.

Account Information includes your account ID and password, name, address, email, personal web site, etc.

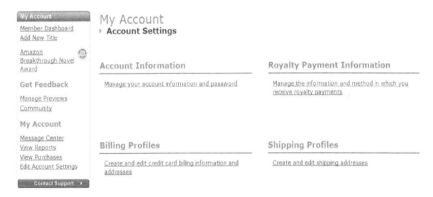

Royalty Payment Information deals with where you want your cheques sent to, or, if you live in the States, the bank account information where you want your royalties deposited via electronic funds transfers. This is also where your tax information is held. If you're a US citizen royalty payments are treated as regular income and taxes arc deducted at the source. If you live outside the States, taxes of 30% will be withheld at by CreateSpace, unless you have an ITIN number and your home country has a tax exemption treaty with the

States. Click on the Tax Interview Help Guide for more detailed information.

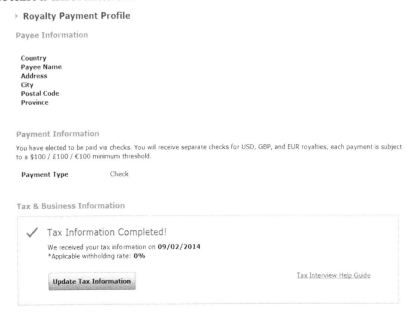

Payments from CreateSpace are paid to a US bank account, or mailed to you as a cheque, whenever there is more than $100 in royalties each of your accounts. Note that CreateSpace sells in three currencies, US dollars ($), UK pounds(£) and European euros(€). Each currency is considered to be a separate account, and sales must exceed 100 in each currency before a cheque for that currency is issued. This means you could be receiving US dollar cheques from US sales, while having 50 pounds or 50 euros sitting dormant in the other accounts.

As mentioned, royalties from sales are considered to be a US revenue stream, as this is a US based company. As such, the publishing company is required to deduct 30% US taxes at the source and to recover those taxes you will need to complete a US tax return.

However, if you are not a US citizen and do not reside in the States you may find that there are tax treaties in effect between the States and your country which can reduce the amount of tax you have to pay. Some examples include:

Canada: 0%   Australia: 5%   U.K.: 0%
Japan: 0%   Germany: 0%   South Africa: 0%

In order to make use of these tax treaties you will need to contact the US tax department and request a US IRS-issued *Individual Taxpayer Identification Number*, referred to as an *ITIN*. This process is fairly involved, though not difficult. I did this through Smashwords as it was the first publisher I began dealing with. They describe the process quite clearly in their help pages and while it was easy to follow it took almost eight months to complete. All companies described in the Zero Cost Series follow the same procedure and all companies must be notified of your ITIN once you have acquired it. You only need one ITIN. You can use any of the companies to complete the process. I won't go into detail, as the process may change over time. I recommend you review the help pages from whichever publisher you chose whenever you are ready to begin the process. In general though, the process is as follows (this is from the Smashwords process which I used).

To acquire an ITIN takes approximately eight months. To begin, you must request a signed letter from the publisher, (CreateSpace) and this can only be requested after your royalties cross a certain threshold as set by the company. To avoid receiving any royalty payments and having taxes deducted during the time you're acquiring the ITIN you should defer all payments by not filling out any payment information. Any royalties earned will simply sit in your account for those eight months. Next, you download the IRS W7 form, complete it and send it to the IRS (check the publishers help pages for the current address to use), along with the hand signed letter from your publisher and a certified copy of your passport. The IRS will then send you an ITIN. This last step took a significant part of the eight months.

You then download a W8-Ben form from the publisher, complete it, showing your ITIN, and send a copy to each of the publishers you have chosen to deal with. Each of the publishers then register your ITIN with their finance department and from then on will provide royalty payments deducting only the amount of taxes required under the tax treaty.

One of the requirements of the IRS to issue an ITIN is a certified copy of your passport. While any notary will make a certified copy of your passport for a fee, ranging from $50 to $100, if you're Canadian you can take your passport down to the passport office and they will make a certified copy for you at no charge. This option takes about three weeks to complete and requires you to surrender your passport for the duration, so don't plan on traveling while you're getting the copy made.

While acquiring an ITIN is a long process and requires filling out a number of forms, I found it was worth pursuing as I had no desire to complete a US tax return every year to get my money back from the IRS.

Remember that royalties from book sales do count as income, so even if you get an ITIN, you should still report your royalty income on your regular annual tax return, regardless of which country you live in.

Sales are reported within a few days of them taking place, and displayed on the *'View Reports'* screen. Below is the summary of all unpaid sales on all titles.

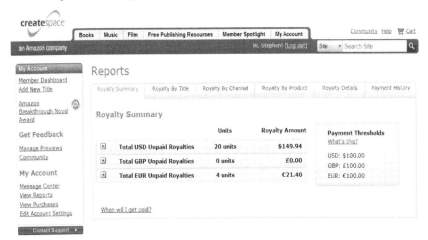

For more detail there are a series of customizable reports providing complete sales information over any given time period. These reports are displayed on screen, but can also be downloaded as an Excel .csv file.

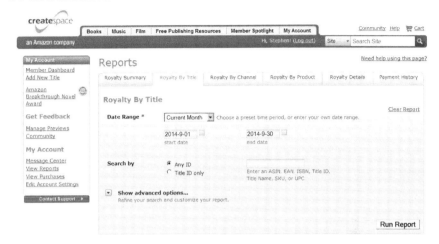

Payment history of cheques sent to you and the sales they cover can also be reported in detail and downloaded as a .csv file.

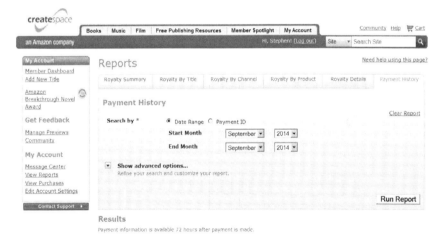

As the author you have the ability to order copies of your books for your own distribution. For example, you might want to sell books at a farmers market. If you give lectures on the book topic you can offer books for sale during the lectures. Any books you order are at the basic production cost and do not count towards your sales royalty figures. You can then sell them at a different cover price, based on the cost of the book plus the cost of shipping to your home address. The *'View Purchases'* option on the left hand menu gives a report on all orders you have placed for books.

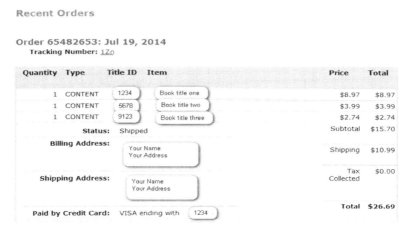

The final options on the menu screen are Billing and Shipping addresses. They can be the same address or you can have a multiple versions of each. You can also keep multiple addresses on file and select the appropriate one when you place the order.

Congratulations again, you're finished. You are now a full fledged author, making sales, earning royalties and receiving income from your book(s).

Technical Complexity: low

Filling out web and paper forms and viewing web browser displays.

Last Words - Next Steps

At this point you have several things of great importance to your creative efforts. First, you have a published, printed book, published by CreateSpace and distributed to the world via CreateSpace, Amazon and other major book reseller sites. Second, you have a master copy of your manuscript, properly formatted and ready for publishing. This could be a Word document, or a document you created with some other word processor, such as Open Office or Libre Office, and saved as a .doc or .docx formatted file. Third, you have a PDF formatted version of the master manuscript.

If your goal was to produce a paper book only, then you're finished. Congratulations. However, you can now take a couple more steps and publish your book in eBook formats. There are two major eBook formats.

The first is the **.epub** format, used by iPhones, Smartphones, all brands of tablets, computers, laptops, Apple devices and various brands of dedicated eBook readers. This is the world generic format, used by all manufacturers and publishers except Amazon. A computer technology company recently reported 175 million tablets were sold in 2013, and predicted more than 300 million would be sold by the end of 2014. It also predicted that over 900 million IPhones and Smartphones would sell in 2014.

The second is the **.mobi** format, for use with Amazon Kindle readers and reader software. As Kindle reader software is also available in the tablet, PC, Mac and Smartphone arenas this isn't as restrictive as it may sound.

This is a huge potential market for eBooks, and one you should be taking advantage of. You already have your book ready to go. You can now publish to epub and mobi using more free tools and companies.

Smashwords is a web based company which specializes in producing **.epub** format eBooks and distributing them to major resellers, including Apple, Barnes & Noble, Kobo, Flipkart and others, including several international library outlets such as 3M Cloud and Overdrive Media.

Amazon KDP is available to publish in **.mobi** format and sell via the Amazon international sites.

There are other 'self-publishing' companies out there but these two are the only ones I've found which, like CreateSpace, provide the tools that allow you to publish your book at no cost, while still providing excellent distribution and royalty payment options.

As this book of the *Zero Cost Self Publishing Series* is aimed specifically at publishing on CreateSpace I'll go no further on eBook production, however, there are other books in the series which cover those topics specifically. Please go to the **Series** web site at:

www.stephencnorton.com/home/zero-cost-publishing-series

and browse the titles for other books of interest.

Thank you for purchasing this book. I hope it proved useful and good luck in all your publishing endeavors.

Notes from the Author

Thank you for reading this book, I hope you enjoyed it, and hope you find it helpful in publishing your own books at zero cost. As a thank you for purchasing this book, you can also purchase the eBook version of the main book **Zero Cost Self Publishing**, containing all the books of the Series, for **20% off** the eBook price. Just browse to https://www.smashwords.com/books/view/258154 to purchase and enter the coupon code **XL29A.** Offer good until December 31, 2015 and may be extended.

~~~~

For access to my other books, or to send comments, please contact me at my web site:

www.StephenCNorton.com

or

email: comment@stephencnorton.com

~~~~

This book was published by
Northwind Ink
Victoria BC
Canada

www.NorthwindInk.com

email: publish@northwindink.com

Northwind Ink is a small Canadian publishing house, specializing in small run editions while providing access to global sales via Amazon and other on-line distributers. We support new authors in most genres and those looking to publish their own memoirs. Our aim is to keep costs to the author as low as possible, while still producing a quality publication. We produce books both you and we can be proud of.

22582047R00040

Printed in Poland
by Amazon Fulfillment
Poland Sp. z o.o., Wrocław